BBC MUSIC GUIDES

———

MAHLER SYMPHONIES AND SONGS

Neil G Walton

BBC MUSIC GUIDES

Mahler Symphonies and Songs

PHILIP BARFORD

BRITISH BROADCASTING CORPORATION

Published by the British Broadcasting Corporation
35 Marylebone High Street, London W1M 4AA

SBN 563 09274 2
First published 1970
© Philip Barford 1970

Printed in England by
Cox & Wyman Ltd, London, Reading and Fakenham

Contents

To Gwynneth

Introduction

In the music of Gustav Mahler romantic feeling and profound lyrical sensibility are exalted to the highest degree. He was a man of philosophical culture, spiritual ideals and quite extraordinary tonal sensitivity. The popularity of his music at the present time raises interesting questions. After half a century during which composers everywhere have reacted against the romantic spirit, sometimes – like Stravinsky – with an almost polemical zeal, Mahler enjoys something like a triumph; his vision of a lyrical and symphonic synthesis of human aspirations appeals to an ever wider audience. Alma Mahler, in retrospect, saw her husband's life almost as a mission. At the end of her *Memories* she writes: 'His battle for the eternal values, his elevation above trivial things and his un-flinching devotion to truth are an example of the saintly life.'

Mahler was in every sense an individualist, with the inherent emotional instability of hypersensitive temperament. Jewish by birth, he embraced Roman Catholicism not least, as Hans Redlich points out in *Bruckner and Mahler*,* because baptism was a regret-tably necessary passport to European culture. Although tempera-mentally drawn to liberal ideals, he was later deeply attracted by Christian mysticism. Basically, his philosophical and religious attitudes took him beyond conventional frameworks of belief; and to call him a humanist is to underestimate his spiritual vision. From some points of view he emerges as a devotee of the free spirit, the kind of man who must ever find his own way under the prompting of spiritual energies awakening in his own soul. Such devotees easily antagonise the orthodox, especially when they give powerful expression to their boundless aspiration.

Life was never easy for Mahler, not only because he frequently found himself in conflict with outward circumstances, but also because of unresolved conflicts within himself. Alma Mahler, in a moving passage in her first book of recollections, describes the death of her first husband as a crucifixion. It seems an apt image. For Mahler's musical temperament seemed to bring all romantic tensions to a crucial focus. It is as if the nineteenth century emptied itself into him, seeking a point of balance, a definitive expression in his work.

* Dent, 1955.

The overall tendency of German music, from Schubert through to Schoenberg, Berg and Webern, has been to heighten the expressive burden not only of melody and chord-progression but of individual moments of sound. With Schubert, the intensification of lyrical progression is often achieved by a master-stroke of major-to-minor modulation: it was also a favourite device of Mahler's, as was also the reverse – minor to major. Schubert was also a lyricist who wrote symphonies, and to some extent the two had common problems, including the establishment of a satisfactory relationship between lyrical expression and symphonic structure.

The intensification of tonal values in Mahler's music arose from a progressive deepening of his lyrical impulse and an increasing sensitivity to the world, a world he loved for its beauty but to which, in terms of human relationship, he could never adjust. What exactly lay behind this deepening? In general terms, the romantic century tried to exalt music as a religion of sensuous beauty. It was Wagner, specifically, who carried this attempt to fantastic lengths, and made music carry the burdens of symbolism (*The Ring*), philosophical ideas (*Tristan*) and mystical ritual (*Parsifal*). The unfolding of a Wagnerian music-drama is not something which can be explained solely in the language of musical analysis. For Wagner, thematic statement fuses tonal image and idea. The development of themes, not only in terms of structure, but also through exotic orchestral colouring and rich harmony, therefore amounts to a tonal exploration of symbol, image and idea.

As the romantic century deepened its interior consciousness through intensification of the sound-symbol, enrichment of the orchestral palette and increasing harmonic resource, the psychological problem inherent in romanticism came to the fore. Romantic music could convey supremely well the longing of finite man for the joys of a boundless *Eros*; but having done this it could not satisfy the soul's thirst for reality. Hence the music-dramas of Wagner, the songs and early symphonies of Mahler now seem to us to exist in a realm of romantic dreaming. Later Mahler's idealism is tempered by personal suffering. He became increasingly aware of conflict between the ideal and the actual. The tragic note sounded so often in his last songs and symphonies reveals his sense of identity with the tragic theme of life, the endless frustration of human aspirations.

8

Increasingly passionate emphasis upon the expressive values of sound in order to convey the consciousness of spiritual conditions inevitably brought about a tonal break-through to the unconscious; and it is against this background that the subsequent development of German expressionism should be considered. The period coincided with the emergence of Freudian psychology. Mahler himself, towards the end of his life, was one of Freud's patients. Romanticism ultimately exacerbated the plane of emotion; and it is frequently through the intensification of emotion that various forms of psychism, either neurotic or religious, eventually appear. For a time Schoenberg himself was attracted by the visionary mysticism of Swedenborg. The decay of romanticism and the new psychological awareness account for significant features of Mahler's musical idiom which is by turns idealistic, ironic, tragic and death-conscious.

Throughout his music, whether symphonic settings of idealistic texts or earth-bound funeral marches which mourn all too realistically the universality of human suffering and our common end, the extreme sensitivity of his tonal expression invites description as 'tonal psychism'. This would apply to moments of tremendous intensity, when the lyrical impulse is focused in sounds which carry an expressionistic overload, a great burden of meaning, significance and emotional pressure. Such moments are found in the *Kindertotenlieder*, the Chorus Mysticus of the Eighth Symphony, even on the first page of the First Symphony, to give but three examples. Heightened tonal utterance is a hall-mark of Mahler's style, a feature which deepens the sound of his orchestra to a peculiar intensity; a telling example is the solemn and arresting low C which opens 'Der Abschied', the last movement of *Das Lied von der Erde*. It is coloured by double-bass, cello, harp, tamtam, horn and double-bassoon, one of the most fertile strokes of musical imagination in the whole work. To listen to a Mahler symphony is to have not only a musical experience but to be profoundly stirred in psycho-spiritual inwardness by an emotionally highly-charged sound-pattern. There can be no doubt that Mahler strove to achieve precisely this disturbing effect – a 'shattering effect' as he once described it after a performance of the Second Symphony. He wanted his listeners to apprehend the depth of life in the way he experienced it, in joy and sorrow, aspiration, longing, resignation. A symphony by Mahler, as he himself put it, is a *world*; and in Mahler's symphonic worlds all kinds of elements drawn from different facets of human experience find musical expression. This is particularly true of the Second, Third and Fourth Symphonies, where settings of religious songs from *Des Knaben Wunderhorn*, a famous collection of folk-poetry made by Clemens Brentano and Achim von Arnim, are found side by side with purely instrumental movements.

Mahler's concern with transcendence is apparent again and again. It is obvious, for example, in the Second Symphony, which begins with a tragically coloured first movement, and works through two succeeding movements to a setting of 'Urlicht' from *Des Knaben Wunderhorn,* the gist of which is the affirmation of an inner light which leads the lost soul of man to God. Following a tortuous instrumental section, the Symphony ends with an overwhelming choral setting of Klopstock's resurrection hymn, 'Auferstehen', which Mahler had heard at Hans von Bülow's funeral. Similar 'evolutionary' developments through a sequence of associated movements can be traced in the Third, Fourth and Eighth symphonies. This drive is not always consciously organised in terms of systematic thematic manipulation. The movements tend to be linked more by a technique of inspired image-association reinforced by thematic cross-references. In the Second Symphony, for instance, the third movement is really a symphonic enhancement of the original accompaniment to an independently composed song, 'St Anthony and the Fishes'. The irony of the poem is transferred, by implicit association, to the orchestral transcription, and is significant in the context of the symphony as a whole. In the Eighth Symphony, thematic cross-references underline poetic and philosophical interconnections linking the ancient hymn 'Veni Creator Spiritus' with the last scene of the Second Part of Goethe's *Faust*.

There is, however, a far more subtle thread which links the movements of Mahler's symphonies and which can be traced in almost everything he wrote. Here is the archetype of a basic shape, a characteristic curve of melodic flow which dominated Mahler's lyrical inspiration:

Ex. 1

This shape is susceptible of almost infinite variation. It is found in some of the songs and all the symphonies. It appears in simple, uncomplicated structures, and is sometimes, especially in the later symphonies, masked by chromatic elaboration. The parent figure yields subsidiary shapes by inversion, retrogression and fragmentation, all of which play parts of thematic importance in Mahler's works. A further point is that the basic shape as given in Ex. 1 is contained in the chord of the 'added sixth', which plays an important part in the closing pages of *Das Lied von der Erde*:

Ex. 2

These haunting sounds contradict the triumphant affirmations of the Eighth Symphony composed only a short time before, and ring the death-knell of romantic aspiration in Mahler's music.

The Songs

Mahler's songs are among his best-loved compositions. They fall into five main groups, apart from a few separate pieces, and with relatively few exceptions the more famous are characterised by nostalgic and sombre reflection upon different facets of life.

The earliest group, *Lieder und Gesänge aus der Jugendzeit,* consists of fourteen songs for voice and piano, and was published in three books in 1885 and 1892. These are youthful works; but they reveal Mahler's love for *Des Knaben Wunderhorn*. This remained undiminished for a great part of Mahler's life, and gave unending inspiration for many fine songs. Indeed, so marked is this influence that *Des Knaben Wunderhorn* provided ideas and programmatic associations for symphonic movements, especially in the Second, Third and Fourth Symphonies – which are consequently known as the *Wunderhorn* symphonies. There was an emotional and spiritual kinship between the content of the poems, their mood and atmosphere, and Mahler's own romantic and mystical temperament. *Lieder und Gesänge* are interesting mainly because they contain thematic material used later in the *Wunderhorn* symphonies. Richard Leander's German translation of Tirso de Molina's *Don Juan* supplemented *Wunderhorn* texts and provided poems for Book I, together with *Hans und Grete,* a text written by Mahler himself. The second and third books consist entirely of *Wunderhorn* songs.

LIEDER EINES FAHRENDEN GESELLEN

On a much higher level of artistic achievement are the *Lieder eines fahrenden Gesellen* (Songs of a Wayfarer) for voice and orchestra, composed between 1883 and 1885, and published in 1897. The occasion for their composition was an experience very similar to the romantic situation depicted in Schubert's *Die Winterreise*: a lonely wanderer setting out for nowhere in particular after a desperately unhappy love-affair. The lady in the case was the actress Johanne Richter, whose blue eyes captivated the composer and gave him much pain. In the text of these songs, Mahler wore his heart upon his sleeve, and he later expressed anxiety lest his verses should be thought too naïve in their emotional fervour.

A quaintly mournful little phrase in D minor for clarinets accompanied by harp opens the first song. After two unembellished statements, it appears for the third time, augmented, as the first vocal phrase. This interplay between the curling figure of accompaniment and its extension in longer notes by the singer is prolonged, and it forms the outer framework enclosing a contrasting middle section. Despite the heavily-loaded expression of a lover bemoaning the marriage of the beloved to someone else, the composer avoids what Hans Redlich* calls 'the sweltering harmonies of late Wagner', and 'the psychological ponderousness of Brahms'. Mahler's orchestral palette is organised here on chamber-music lines, with plain harmonies and exceptionally clear colouring. The overall mood is set by the simplest devices – a turn of five notes, repeated fifths in the bass, and uncomplicated folk-like melody. Quite marked in the first song is the interval of the fourth, which plays an important part in the First Symphony, and which the composer increasingly exploits for its astringent harmonic effects:

Ex. 3

The second song, 'Ging heut' morgens übers Feld', supplied material for the first movement of the First Symphony, and evolves most beautifully from the descending fourth of the opening tune:

Ex. 4

Fourths also figure importantly in the harmony. Half-way through, the key changes exquisitely to B major, throwing an ethereal gleam over the pastoral bliss described in the first lines of the song. The world is full of light; but will the singer's happiness return? Unfortunately, no.

The third song, *schnell und wild,* with its stark, almost brutal, note of desperation, begins in D minor ('I have a glowing dagger in my breast'), but yields to a tender, characteristically Mahlerian interlude in C major as the composer likens the blue of heaven above to the eyes of the beloved. The tension of the first section is increased by a dramatic conclusion in E flat minor. (This chromatic intensification of tonality is exploited to wonderful effect in the first movement of *The Song of the Earth*.)

* Introduction to the Eulenburg score.

No. 4 begins with a funeral march in E minor, and like the preceding song ends a semitone higher (in F minor); and it will be noticed that its opening key is a semitone higher than the ending of the previous song. The vocal line is extremely simple throughout, and phrased in slow, sad sections. The instrumental colouring of the accompaniment is a wonderful stroke of imagination, the mood being set by three low flutes, cor anglais, clarinets and harp. Towards the end a gentle folk-like melody, beginning in F major and slowly yielding to the minor, is introduced with haunting arpeggios. This section reappears in the slow movement of the First Symphony. Along with the 'wayfarer' image in the nineteenth century goes that of the lime tree. At this point the wayfarer, like his predecessor in Schubert's *Winter Journey,* lies down to sleep, and is gently covered by linden blossom. Flutes and harp return with final statements of the funereal opening rhythm.

Mahler's highly original and richly colouristic style of orchestral song accompaniment is continued in twelve *Wunderhorn* songs published in 1905. These are a very varied selection, and two of them are found in the Second Symphony. 'Urlicht', which was originally conceived in the framework of the Symphony, sings of man's 'nameless need', and of God who will give man a guiding light leading him to unending bliss. The song rises to an ecstatic peak of lyrical expression in its final phrase, which is related to the basic shape already mentioned (Ex. 1). The entry of the contralto voice after the instrumental third movement of the Symphony is unforgettable; but the song is also wonderfully effective as a separate piece. Perhaps it unites romantic longing with mystical aspiration as perfectly as any other work in the composer's output. 'Wo die schönen Trompeten blasen' invokes a Housman mood in its picture of the soldier making his farewells before leaving for distant lands – there to find his bed of green grass within the sound of shining trumpets. This song opens softly in D minor with melancholy fourths and a well-known trumpet call; but the mood is wonderfully transfigured by a Schubertian switch to the major key as the soldier addresses his sleeping beloved.

After a brief return to D minor there is another change, this time to G flat major for a central episode. The music returns once more to D major before ending in the minor. What this moving piece reveals is Mahler's characteristic method of structural association, whereby passages in different key-colours establish a deeply affecting musical and emotional pattern. It is interesting to reflect how far Mahler, who was always impatient of having his work analysed, conceived the structural unity of his composition as a unity of associated sound-images. He stands always at the emotional and spiritual centre of groups of sound-images, intuitively linking keys, themes and harmonies in refreshingly original ways – although Donald Mitchell remarks on possible precedents for this in the songs of Schumann.* The archetype frequently found in Mahler's textures (Ex. 1), quite apart from its structural force, symbolically suggests an emotional and spiritual centre adopted almost instinctively as a melodic stance. His sympathetic penetration of *Wunderhorn* texts is bound up with this.

KINDERTOTENLIEDER

In the *Kindertotenlieder* (Dirges for Children) we sense a deepened psychological insight, intensified chromatic inflection, and a fascinating orchestration which develops the chamber style of the *Wayfarer* songs. The poems are by Friedrich Rückert, and Mahler confessed, after the death of his elder daughter, that he had set them 'in an agony of fear lest this should happen'. Such music is thus the fervent outpouring of one to whom every moment of happiness is tinged with darkness, every moment of joy a threat of future pain, and every optimistic promise dubious of realisation. It exactly reveals the secret apprehensions of a mother anxious about her children, and that Mahler should have been moved to set such tragic poems is evidence of his character. According to Richard Specht, Mahler appeared to believe that his own artistic creations amounted to a prophetic anticipation of future events. In a similar vein of apprehension, he regarded his Ninth Symphony as a foreshadowing of his own death. The hammer-blows in the Sixth also had prophetic force. To some this must seem a regrettable neurosis; others may feel that composition and performance of such deeply-felt music is indeed a sort of ritual pre-enactment. Whatever the truth, these dark songs are a clue to the deepest levels of Mahler's musical personality. Their melodic inspiration is more free from the gravitational pull of Ex. 1 than most other compositions. For

* *Gustav Mahler. The Early Years* (Rockliff, 1958).

the most part attention is fixed by the subtle and profoundly expressive use of chromatically inflected melody, supported by a counterpoint of expressive orchestral figuration overwhelming in its effect. In the *Kindertotenlieder* Mahler does not shrink from the most compelling use of tonal psychism. His music relentlessly probes subconscious fears.

Contemporary with the *Kindertotenlieder,* composed between 1901 and 1904, were five more settings of poems by Rückert. The group has close emotional and thematic affinities with *Das Lied von der Erde,* composed during 1907-08, and the songs often follow the basic shape of Ex. 1 fairly closely. The following example is from 'Ich bin der Welt abhanden gekommen', which extols the joys of life in the country given up to poetry and love – a life which Mahler idealised in music but could never, as a musical director committed to the pressure of endless travel and rehearsals, enjoy for more than short spells in the summer. Notice the very characteristic curve of these phrases:

Ex. 5

and compare this vocal line from 'Der Abschied' in *Das Lied von der Erde*:

Ex. 6

16

sein   zum   letz - ten   Le   -   be - wohl.

An anticipatory glance through the score of *Das Lied* at this point will reveal how Mahler, in what is probably his greatest work, committed himself wholeheartedly to this type of melodic structure, for large sections are entirely based upon it. It is as if the resignation to which all critics refer when discussing the psychological ethos of *The Song*, and which is also a mark of the last songs, was as much resignation to the inner force of a recurring thematic motivation as it was to the collapse of the romantic consciousness in its struggle to transcend itself in mystical realisation. Was this basic shape the very essence of Mahler himself? Certainly Mahler is never more at home with his material than he is in the vocal line of *Das Lied* and the Rückert songs. These examples all show close thematic affinities:

Ex. 7

(i)

Ich   at - me leis ____   im Duft   der   Lin   -   de

(ii)

O nicht mich   Lie - be!   Lie - be die Son - ne

(iii)

O   Menschheit dei - ner   Lei   -   -   den

The theme of resignation is made explicit in the sad but beautiful 'Um Mitternacht'. No strings are used in this song, and the dark-toned colouring of the orchestra is enhanced by bass tuba, trombones, oboe d'amore and double bassoon. The poet sings of his desolation during the midnight hour when, after contemplation of the sufferings of mankind, he resigns all power to God. For Mahler this must have been a deeply significant song. Midnight darkness always awakened powerful emotions. Earlier he had been stirred by the midnight warning of Nietzsche's Zarathustra which he had given a central position in the Third Symphony.

To know Mahler's music it is necessary to know his songs intimately, and to appreciate the interplay between vocal line and orchestral accompaniment. This accompaniment is not figuration alone but a subtle, ever-shifting structure of planes of colour. The vocal line is frequently interrupted by short orchestral 'interludes'; but these are basic to the wholeness of the form, which is expressed in a pattern of associated images. The poetry of the sung line is thus offset by sound-clusters which surround and colour the melodic phrases with haunting overtones of purely orchestral expression. When the voice is silent, the orchestra explores its soul.

On the other hand, Mahler proclaimed that he always reached a stage in purely instrumental composition when the need to bring in the voice became imperative. The fact seems to be that his creative urge was essentially lyrical, and some of his most satisfying symphonic writing paradoxically grows out of this lyrical impulse. To sing is to utter images and ideas; and images and ideas have their own interior logic of association and structural implication. Mahler nourished his musical invention on images and world-embracing ideas, and in this way discovered fascinating sound-structures.

Symphony No. 1 in D

The First Symphony in D major is Mahler's first enduring contribution to the repertoire of major concert works. It was begun in 1884 in Kassel, completed in 1888 at Leipzig, and first performed at Budapest in 1889. Aiming as always at the utmost clarity, Mahler revised the instrumentation before it was published in Vienna in 1899. Originally the Symphony had five movements, the extra one being an *andante* between the first movement and scherzo. This was later dropped, together with a programme very freely derived from Jean Paul Richter's novel *The Titan*:

Part I. From the days of youth, youth-, fruit- and thorn-pieces.
   1. Spring and no end. The introduction depicts the awakening of nature at earliest dawn.
   2. Flower chapter (*andante*).
   3. Full sail (scherzo).

Part II.   Commedia umana.

   4. Shipwrecked. A funeral march in Callot's manner (The
      Hunter's Funeral: Weimar). The following may, *if necessary*,
      serve as explanation: the external impulse to this piece was
      given the composer by the parodistic picture, 'The Hunter's
      Funeral', well known to all children in South Germany from
      an old book of fairy-tales: the forest animals follow the
      hunter's coffin; hares carry the pennon, a band of Bohemian
      musicians goes in front, accompanied by cats, toads, crows,
      etc., playing instruments, and stags, roe-deer, foxes and other
      four-legged and feathered creatures of the woods follow the
      procession in comic attitudes. Here this piece is to be thought
      of as the *expression* of a mood sometimes of ironical merriment,
      sometimes of sinister brooding, followed immediately by

   5. Dall' inferno al Paradiso (*allegro furioso*), the sudden expression
      of a heart wounded to its depths.

The Symphony is programmatic in that it evolves an experience
through explicit stages. Part I expounds youthful hopes, memories
and the promise of bliss. Part II depicts what happens after an
emotional crisis. In the slow movement there is tragedy; and in so
far as irony, cynicism and self-mockery can be imputed to patterns
of sound, these are also present. The triumphant finale overcomes
them with what some might feel to be a rather desperate and
simple-minded heroism. The Symphony's relationship to the
Wayfarer cycle has already been noted. In fact, the work has a
complex background of emotional entanglement. The *Wayfarer*
songs, on which Mahler was working whilst composing the
Symphony, refer to the affair with Johanne Richter; but in 1886, in
Leipzig, he also fell passionately in love with the wife of Weber's
grandson, a much older woman. In an emotional sense, the
Symphony is essentially a 'wayfarer' symphony, with every traditional aspect of the 'wayfarer' image underlined in music of
tremendous variety and colour.

The beginning of the first movement is one of the loveliest
symphonic openings in romantic music – a sustained high-octave
A which sets a mood of ethereal pastoral contemplation. Mahler's
A is the as yet unformed space of a spring dawn, and it gradually
unfolds a sequence of descending fourths. These anticipate the
descending fourth of 'Ging heut' morgens übers Feld', which

19

emerges from the texture with a delicious sense of uninhibited freedom. They also provide 'cuckoo' motives, although Mahler's cuckoo sings in perfect fourths and not, like Delius's, in minor thirds. Eventually, with the help of hunting fanfares, and orchestration abounding in sheer *joie de vivre*, the morning song breaks out into ebullient ecstasy. Throughout the movement it supplies much of the melodic material; but the vitality and fascination of the structural scheme owe much to short subsidiary figures – horn calls, the cuckoo motive, and repeated curling sequences which float inconsequentially about the score. Perhaps the most beautiful and affecting part of the movement is the recapitulation. Here the high A is sustained for many bars, and gradually wanes out to *pppp* before descending gently down the arpeggio of D major to the accompaniment of bird calls (flute) and distant horn chords. Mahler must have liked this effect because something very similar recurs in the first movement of the Third Symphony, sparked off, no doubt, by the common association of elemental life.

The finale is thematically related to the first movement, and after preliminary shrieks of despair soon settles down to develop a figure developed from it:

Ex. 8

(i) First movement

(ii) Finale

The three upward steps become the foundation of assertive, muscular counterpoint later on. Also important is the triumphant chorale theme, finally blasted out on trombones. This obviously derives from the descending fourths of the first movement, and reveals the underlying unity of invention linking the beginning and ending of the Symphony. For many listeners the most affecting part of the finale may well be this sentimental interlude:

Ex. 9

Sehr langsam

An exuberant waltz-scherzo and a slow movement, based upon 'Frère Jacques', played in canon in D minor, and the folk-like melody heard in the last *Wayfarer* song, constitute the two central movements. There is much play upon the tonic and dominant notes which are foreshadowed in the descending fourths of the first movement. These set the dance rhythm of the waltz and the plodding tempo of the funeral march; they also feature in the last *Wayfarer* song.

The strange-sounding, highly original music of the funeral march retains its fascination today. It contains cynical parodies of the sound of a marching band which enhance the grotesquerie of the whole movement. Apparently Mahler, as a child, was frequently wheeled in his pram to a neighbouring barracks where his nurse had a soldier sweetheart; military fanfares and rhythms would thus be among his earliest musical impressions. It is entirely likely that the association with 'Frère Jacques' occurred simply because his nurse used to sing the tune while waiting outside the barracks. In any case, the sound of the marching band was a very familiar one in nineteenth-century Austria, and all popular composers of dance music churned out military marches by the dozen. Right at the end of Mahler's piece the bassoon quotes a figure which plays a prominent part in the song 'Wo die schönen Trompeten blasen'. English listeners who have served in the forces will find it has a familiar sound. Plodding fourths have the last word.

The Symphony was never really popular in Mahler's lifetime. To many musicians at the turn of the century it must have seemed backward-looking, relying too much upon outdated romantic gestures, heroic postures, and the well-worn theme of the hero winning through against odds. There are certainly tedious moments in the finale, which is naïve in its quotations from the first movement, its repetitious assertion of triumph, and curiously trite on its last chord. Even so, its poetry and tone-painting and its store of romantic themes have established it as a favourite.

The Wunderhorn Symphonies

In the Second, Third and Fourth Symphonies Mahler explored a world of sound to which the voice adds dimensions of explicit meaning and association. These confirm Mahler's belief, once expressed in a letter, that the man of letters, the philosopher and the painter are all integrated in the musician. Mahler himself had been a student of philosophy, and he also wrote poetry. Such a belief foreshadowed Schoenberg's subsequent affirmation that 'music expresses the unconscious nature of this and other worlds'. It is significant that Schoenberg, a devoted admirer of Mahler, was also a painter with a great interest in the relations between images, ideas and sounds, an interest supremely vindicated in his unfinished opera *Moses und Aron*. In that great work images are governed by ideas, and the framework of ideas is ordered by a single 'master-concept' symbolised in a tone-row. 'Grant you now,' says Moses to Aron, 'the power of idea over word and image?' Much the same could be said of Mahler's *Wunderhorn* symphonies. They are rich in associated imagery; but the images convey ideas, and the ideas are arranged according to an overall guiding concept. This gives rise to what might be called 'philosophical listening' – an enjoyment of the tonal structure in the light of the concept. An insight into the guiding concept may take some time to develop. In my own experience, the sound-patterns, fused with associated imagery and ideas, always point forcefully to the ruling concept, so it becomes important to assess what was obviously an inspirational motivation in the composer.

The three *Wunderhorn* symphonies were all furnished with programmatic explanations withdrawn after their first performances. Understandably, Mahler wished to be known as a composer who worked with notes, who was independent of non-musical material, whose symphonies were tonal structures and not mere sound-frameworks for images and ideas. The relation between images, philosophic content and sound can be argued endlessly, raising problems which nobody has finally settled. It is a very live issue in contemporary music. What we could bear in mind is that the quality and range of a composer's experience are bound to find some sort of expression in his works. Between purely abstract patterns which have no explicit relation to any definable idea or visual image, and themes or progressions which carry an explicit symbolic burden, there are many grades of subtle relationship. Perhaps we could accept that whereas some composers work at a great distance of abstraction from those life-experiences which are inspirational to their work, others instinctively transmute the vibration of every passing mood, emotion or aspiration into sound-patterns.

Mahler exposed his musical faculty to anything in human experience which moved him emotionally, although we can detect certain constant preoccupations – the great issues of life, death and love, and the possibility of transmuting one state of consciousness into another. In the background of his mind there seems always to be the image of a ladder up which humanity can climb to heaven. Such an image was given a particular slant by Schoenberg in *Die Jakobsleiter*. External conditions were all experienced by Mahler as part of what Jung later called 'the psychic continuum'. It is interesting that Ernst Kurth (1886–1946), whose theoretical writings had a close relationship to his experience of romantic music, stressed the importance of the *unheard* musical function, the subjective force which alone gave life to 'dead' sounds. Mahler's best music always sounds as if a powerful flow in his psychic being has turned itself into sound. It is precisely this aspect of 'flow' which finds an important place in Kurth's theories. Recognising the powerful subjective forces flowing through Mahler's music, the young Schoenberg wrote enthusiastically to Mahler after a performance of the Fourth Symphony to say that he had 'seen his soul'. Modern English listeners may have some difficulty in understanding the enthusiasm with which German romantics discussed their souls. The fact remains that we cannot enter into Mahler's musical world unless we are prepared to come to terms with his encompassing aura of belief, doubt, aspiration and emotional reactions. The inner world was a relentless pressure upon him, the hidden scaffolding of his musical flow, the foundation of his symphonic structures. And it may well have been the case that without the emotional drive of an overwhelming experience, the potent suggestion of images, or the force of a philosophical scheme, Mahler would have lacked the vital dimension of his creative genius.

The *Wunderhorn* symphonies are all other-worldly. They unashamedly proclaim faith in love, redemption and the life in heaven. In each case spiritual optimism is expressed in a song from the *Wunderhorn* anthology. The Second Symphony adds a setting of Klopstock's 'Auferstehen' (Resurrection Ode), and the Third a passage from *Zarathustra*, which somewhat offsets the overall mood of confidence to reveal what Bruno Walter called 'the nocturnal element' in Mahler.

SYMPHONY NO. 2 IN C MINOR

The Second, or 'Resurrection' Symphony as it is now known, was the work which convinced Walter that he had found a vocation in conducting Mahler's music. Its effect upon him was overwhelming. It can be equally overwhelming today. Mahler always requires, and nowhere more than in this massive work, that the listener should give himself up completely to the tapestry of sound and idea which the Symphony weaves around him. The overall scheme is not unlike Beethoven's Ninth Symphony, although its psychological atmosphere is different, being deepened by Mahler's uncanny evocation of subjective states associated with death and a passionately individualistic view of resurrection, made explicit by additions to Klopstock's lines. If Beethoven's first movement seems to scan the cosmic drama of life unfolding from a bare, vibrating fifth, Mahler's, erupting from a vicious tremolo, portrays the funeral rites of a hero. In fact, the composer referred to the first movement as 'funeral rites', and the hero as the Titan of the First Symphony. He also claimed that this movement raised the question: 'To what purpose have you lived?' and that the last movement gives the answer. The Symphony (completed on 25 July 1894) is thus a death-and-transfiguration drama. Understandably it interested Richard Strauss, whose tone-poem *Death and Transfiguration* had been composed in 1889, and who conducted the first three movements in Berlin before the first complete performance of the Symphony under Mahler himself.

The next two movements are both in triple tempo, the first being a sophisticated *Ländler*, the second an orchestral transcription of the song 'St Anthony and the Fishes'. The *Ländler* is extraordinarily beautiful and far more delicately precise in its rhythms than the *Ländler* of Schubert and Josef Lanner, the spirit of which it evokes and symphonically transmutes. It is held to be a memory of the past; but its wistful mood is cynically dispelled by St Anthony's experience with the fish. The Viennese illusion fades and life reveals its bitterness, the orchestra providing cynical background noises. How, it seems to imply, can we linger with the memories of care-free youth when life has to be redeemed and regenerated? In this movement the associations of the song penetrate the musical experience. The whirling of the texture and the acid colouring of the score lead, as Mahler intends that they should, to feelings of restlessness and disillusion.

After the scherzo has died away with hollow, cheerless sounds, Mahler introduces the voice with the song 'Urlicht'. The entry of the contralto on the words 'O Röschen rot' is unforgettable, and it serves as a pivotal point transfiguring the symphonic scheme with light and depth. The poem is a strange one, naïve in symbolism and profound in implication. It can be read in the light of Psalm 18, verse 28. Is the mystical rose an allusion to the Rose of Sharon, or the rose in Christian symbolism which has traditionally been associated with both Jesus Christ and the Virgin Mary? A German title of Mary is 'Marien Röselen'. Dante, in the *Paradiso,* Canto XXII, refers to the Rose in which the Logos became incarnate. The symbolism is clear: there is an inner light of the soul which will lead mankind out of death into the light of God. The orchestra accompanies the words with solemn, sustained brass harmonies and angelic tinklings.

Immediately after the song, which ends with the voice climbing ecstatically to the tonic through Mahler's favourite ascending curve, there is a tempestuous outburst of orchestral sound. Here the parallel with Beethoven's Ninth is unmistakable – confident, spiritualistic aspiration shattered by dissonant harmonies and strident orchestration. The agonised orchestral development which follows is very difficult to conduct, being susceptible of endless variety of interpretation. Klemperer's different recordings of this part vary astoundingly. This is because the texture weaves together an elaborate kaleidoscope of tonal images, quoting the march theme from the first movement, and anticipating passages from the chorale on Klopstock's 'Auferstehen' which is to follow – and all with striking dynamic contrasts and fluctuations of tempo. An example is the passionate, even agonising, figure associated in the finale with the solo contralto singing 'O glaube, mein Herz, O glaube' (O believe, my heart, believe). Against a background of tremolo flutes, English horn and oboe declaim the vocal phrase with passionate inflections and desperate urgency – exactly as if the difficulty of belief and yet its vital necessity are experienced as an emotional religious crisis. Least satisfactory in the whole long transition to the chorale is the naïve-sounding march music based on Thomas of Celano's famous sequence 'Dies irae'. In due course an ascending stepwise figure heralds the entry of the chorale. Before the voices enter, horns and brass, positioned outside the orchestra, suggest Gabriel's summoning of the legions of the dead. There are strange twitterings on flute and piccolo, and rhythmic movement is suspended in awe-inspiring contemplation of the abyss between earth and heaven. The choral finale is completely convincing, and it reaches a tremendous climax with orchestra and voices mounting wave on wave to their final chord. Here again Mahler's basic shape serves as a structural and thematic backbone, and finds one of its greatest expressions as a theme of aspiration, faith and spiritual triumph. The culmination of this movement should be compared with the Chorus Mysticus of the Eighth Symphony, which employs the same technique on an even grander scale.

There is much fine music in this work, and especially in the first movement, which introduces a fertile succession of themes as the basis of an extended sonata-form scheme. The first themes, centred on C minor, are bound together by common structural features, as well as by their sombre, even sinister, mood, and they are introduced by the strings with protean strength. The second subject is an ascending curve (compare the end of the transition leading to the resurrection hymn) and has some similarities with the transfiguration theme in Strauss's tone-poem. It subsequently reappears in E major with broadening effect. The same remote key also emerges significantly in later movements, and especially in the third where it is associated with a lyrical, expansive and anticipatory theme. It is in the first movement that we hear first the 'Dies irae' march music. Structurally the entire work is cross-referenced with themes which have symbolic force, so it coheres very well in the experience of those who detect the gradual unfolding of the resurrection motive in the programmatic context of death and man's need of God. The sound of a large choir whispering 'Auferstehen' is pure inspiration. Being on a different plane from the march music, which sounds almost simple-minded to modern ears, it is tremendously impressive in its strange intensity. We may remember that the Symphony antedated the horrors of the First World War by only a few years. Mahler's passionate, wish-fulfilling vision of resurrection and his identification with suffering mankind throw prophetic light on the whitened bones of human experience in the twentieth century. From this standpoint, and quite apart from concluding expressions of faith and optimism, it is one of the greatest death-symphonies ever written, especially as it retains a universal reference lost in the agonised introspection of the Ninth Symphony, in which Mahler contemplates his own approaching end.

SYMPHONY NO. 3 IN D MINOR

The Third Symphony, perhaps more than any other work by Mahler, shows his *Gestalt* approach both to human experience and to symphonic structure. Musically it fuses different stylistic levels. Programmatically it knits together a wealth of ideas and associations. It was published in 1902 and first performed complete, under the composer's direction, at Krefeld in June of that year. Weingartner had previously conducted three movements in Berlin, where they had not been well received.

The Symphony was first entitled *The Joyful Science* (after Nietzsche's book, *Die fröhliche Wissenschaft*), and subtitled 'A Summer Morning's Dream', and there is reference to it in a letter of 29 August 1895. The work was finished on 6 August 1896, and in its original form it included as its seventh movement the setting of a *Wunderhorn* song, 'Wir geniessen die himmlischen Freuden', which later became the finale of the Fourth Symphony. Much of the material in the Fourth is foreshadowed in this concluding song; and this throws interesting light upon Mahler's creative processes. It suggests that composition grew out of a continuous chain of interwoven tonal and philosophical fantasy in such a way that one work could begin where another left off. Subconsciously the *Gestalt* tendency in Mahler's mind underlay a predisposition to experience the world whole, to see patterns and connecting links everywhere. In philosophy this same tendency found expression in the nineteenth century in Hegel's metaphysical idealism; but it is a binding-thread in the religious mysticism of all ages.

There is uncertainty about the chain of ideas associated with the Symphony's six movements, and Mahler never publicly divulged its innermost meaning. Lawrence Gilman refers in a programme note* to a conversation he had with his friend Willem Mengelberg, to whom Mahler had once made known the Symphony's 'real programme'. According to Mengelberg, the Symphony has deep humanistic content and sets out to project something of the vision of brotherhood expressed in Beethoven's Ninth. However, as Hans Redlich pointed out,† there are at least five different drafts of the programme. Quite apart from wishing to be known as a 'pure musician', Mahler evidently had some difficulty in rationalising his scheme *after* the event. His *Summer Morning Dream*, as we now know it, is in six movements, which have the following titles:

I Summer marches in.

II What the flowers of the meadow tell me.

III What the animals of the forest tell me.

IV What night tells me (contralto solo, setting words from *Zarathustra*).

V What the morning bells tell me (choir of women and boys

* *Orchestral Music* (Oxford, 1951).
† *Bruckner and Mahler* (Dent, 1955).

with contralto solo, setting words from *Des Knaben Wunder-horn*), and

VI What love tells me.

Mahler indicated that these titles are 'small pointers'.

The first movement is extremely long, and it begins with an exhilarating theme blasted out on eight horns – one of the most exciting beginnings in any nineteenth-century symphony:

Ex. 10

According to Alma Mahler, the movement, which swirls with elemental feeling, depicts the composer's reactions to the awakening of Pan, which he experienced at noonday outside his hut above the house where the family lived at Steinbach during the summer months, and where the composer gave himself up to creative work after the stress of concert-direction during the winter. It was when he stood before this hut, which was characteristically furnished with piano, volumes of Kant and Goethe, and music of Bach, that the inspiration for the Symphony welled up in a rush of sound-images. The experience seems to have been a deeply moving one, and the internal evidence of the music suggests that he felt a mystical unity with the elemental forces of the earth in every nerve and cell. Bruno Walter went to stay with Mahler shortly after completion of the work. When he glanced round at the glorious scenery on his way to the house, the composer said: 'No need to look. I have composed all this already!' Walter was deeply impressed by the music, and it is worth quoting his first reactions:

Thanks to our talks, full of the overflow of the creative frenzy of his morning's work, I was familiar with the spiritual atmosphere of the Symphony long before I knew its musical content. Yet it was a shattering experience to hear him play it at the piano. . . . This music made me feel I recognised him for the first time; his whole being seemed to breathe a mysterious affinity with the forces of nature. I had already guessed its depths, its elemental quality; now, in the range of his creativity, I felt it directly. . . . I saw him as Pan. At the same time, however – this in the last three movements – I was in contact with the longing of the human spirit to pass beyond its earthly and temporal bonds. Light streamed from him on to his work, and from his work on to him.*

Much of the first movement, after the splendid opening and the impressionistic stirrings of the introductory pages, is carried by an ebullient march which co-ordinates in its vigorous rhythms the protean energies of a wealth of thematic material. Unfortunately, as in the Second Symphony, the introduction of march music is not always convincing. Despite its length, the music does not require feats of concentration; yet this is not to deny its power and momentum. Above all, the ear is easily won over by the beauty of the orchestration. Most impressive are the deep brass chords which follow appearances of the initial horn theme.

The movements which follow the conquest of summer over the volcanic eruptions of elemental nature fall easily on the ear also; but they reveal more than ever Mahler's mastery of sound. This is superbly apparent in the delightful *flos campi* music of the second movement, the nostalgic and magically evocative post-horn solo in the third, and the deep-toned colouring of the contralto setting of Nietzsche's words: 'Take heed, O man! The night is deep, and deeper than the day thinks', which are taken from Zarathustra's Second Dance Song where each line in the original is separated by a note of the bell striking the midnight hour. Mahler refrains from depicting this effect literally, substituting instead a sustained and profoundly moving melody to a simple accompaniment. The contralto sings the words 'Gib Acht!' (Take heed) to a falling step, F sharp – E (Ex. 11, i). As the music is in D major, the next downward step would be to the tonic; but this step is not taken, and so the voice hangs suspended, on a note of irresolution. Exactly the same effect occurs in the opening bars of the Ninth Symphony, the first theme of which, also in D major, quotes the same sounds – F sharp – E (Ex. 11, ii). This self-quotation, deliberate or unconscious, reveals much about the symbolic aspect of germinal thematic motives in Mahler's melodies. A further point is that the step of a falling tone also features importantly in setting the word 'Ewig' in

* Bruno Walter, *Gustav Mahler*, trans. Lotte Walter Lindt (Hamish Hamilton, 1958).

the final bars of *Das Lied von der Erde*. The associations in all three cases give food for thought. Nor is this all. Immediately after the Nietzsche setting comes the song of the morning bells, and the cheerful 'Bimm bamm' of young voices resounds to a simple four-note figure (Ex. 11, iii) which also recurs, though in retrograde, in the opening bars of the Ninth Symphony (Ex. 11, iv):

Ex. 11

(i) Symphony III, fourth movement

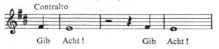

(ii) Symphony IX, first movement

(iii) Symphony III, fifth movement

(iv) Symphony IX, first movement

It forms an ironic counterpoint to that Symphony's opening theme. The way such thematic fragments cross the boundaries between different works, either as literal echoes or mocking self-quotations, is of the greatest musical and psychological interest.

The song of the morning bells is a setting of the *Wunderhorn* poem 'Es sungen drei Engel'. The midnight bells omitted in setting Zarathustra's dance song are here sublimated into the joyful suggestion of light prevailing over darkness – the Johannine light which the 'higher pessimism' associated with Nietzsche and Schopenhauer does not comprehend. In setting Nietzsche in the context of this Symphony, Mahler seems to be at once attracted – like so many romantic artists – by the metaphysical symbol of darkness, and by the warning that things are not what they really seem. In the midst of life we are in death, and the sorrow and tragedy with which it is associated. Nevertheless, the drift of the Third Symphony, clearly implied by the order of the movements (in which we should consider the original placing of the song 'Heavenly Life' which now ends the Fourth Symphony), is to exalt light above darkness, and universal love above the elemental forces of nature. The keynote of Mahler's spiritual optimism is sounded by the morning bells. God is not dead. Love ultimately crowns the pageant of life which began in the primeval stirrings of the earth. In the last movement a flood of glorious music majestically unfolds a magnificent paean of love. It begins with an exquisite instrumental *adagio* deepening and rounding off the entire musical and philosophical conception.

The key-scheme correlative with the order of the movements is interestingly organised. As the Symphony now stands, it begins in D minor and ends in D major. The original conception required it to end in E major, an example of 'progressive tonality'. The unfolding of the formal structure, and the development of the philosophical or religious content step by step to a level of transfigured consciousness in heavenly life finds musical expression in the ascent of one tone. The Symphony was well named when Mahler called it *The Joyful Science*. It is a visionary dream of world harmony, like the one which led Kepler to place the Sun, as the 'throne of God', at the centre of a geometrical system consisting of the five regular Euclidean solids which defined the relative orbits of the planets. For geometrical figures Mahler substituted states of life and consciousness, and even made room for the Abyss, the non-being hinted at in Zarathustra's Night Song. Yet, like Kepler, the composer symbolically elevated the Sun as an ordering principle. It is the solar forces of summer which 'march in' to impose harmony upon the chaos of the elements. To deepen the symbol, it is the divine in man which ultimately masters the flux of creative energies in his soul. Looked at from this point of view, the Symphony offers not only a wonderful pageant of orchestral sounds, but a significantly related series of 'foci' for meditative listening. Also it offers a clue to Mahler's inner preoccupations at this, perhaps the happiest, time of his life. How much these owed to study of Kant and Goethe, whose works provided intellectual food at Steinbach, we shall perhaps never know. We learn from Alma

Mahler that her husband knew the name of every plant and tree in his garden. Did he, perhaps, know Goethe's theory of the 'archetypal plant' which, significantly in relation to the titles of the Third Symphony, lays great stress upon the inwardness of universal formative forces and their oneness with the power of creative imagination in man? And the conclusion of the Symphony with a stream of orchestral polyphony expressing 'What Love tells me' is a suggestive anticipation of the underlying idea of the Eighth, the Symphony of Love, which is based on one of Goethe's seed-ideas, faith in redemption through love. The Third Symphony is a wonderful example of how a richly inspired piece of music can grow from a varied background of images and ideas.

SYMPHONY NO. 4 IN G

The Fourth Symphony (completed in 1900) is the last in which Mahler gave free rein to images associated with the world of the *Wunderhorn,* although these recur rather strangely, and without much conviction, in the middle sections of the Seventh Symphony. The Fourth was published in 1901 and, like all the others, later revised. In terms of texture and structure it marks an advance in musical thinking and symphonic conception. Mahler's melodic gift flowers again, and with wonderful spontaneity, in the deceptively innocent first movement, which is a masterpiece of delicate counterpoint, Mozartian lucidity and sensuous beauty. The second movement, a *Ländler,* is the first example of a type of structure which the composer developed in later works with more acid emphasis. We have already noted his feeling for *Ländler* tempo in the second movement of the 'Resurrection' Symphony. Here it makes its nostalgic point by emphasising an uncomplicated rhythmic accompaniment to the melodic flow. In the *Ländler* of the Fourth, the underlying rhythm is not chained to an over-emphatic one-two-three in the bass but distributed through interwoven parts. The result is one of contrapuntal subtlety, coloured by tightening the strings of the solo violin a whole tone. The composer calls for an effect *wie eine Fiedel,* an evocation of the sound of a street fiddler scraping dance music. The slow movement deepens and dignifies the Symphony with music of profound, meditative beauty. It is one of Mahler's loveliest inspirations, and in moments of impassioned yearning it

C   33

recalls the climbing curve of Ex. 1 which is treated in rising sequences. The last movement has already been mentioned in relation to the Third Symphony. Its most remarkable feature is the modulation to E major near the end. Thus a work which begins in G major is concluded a minor third lower; but the magnetic pull of E is already felt in a theme common to both this Symphony and the Third, where it is heard in the setting of 'Es sungen drei Engel' ('Ich hab' übertreten die zehn Gebot'):

Ex. 12

die Eng - lein, die ba - cken das Brot.

Cross-references between the first movement and the last are found in the chirping fifths with which the work opens, and a similar passage which marks off the strophic divisions of the *Wunderhorn* song. More interesting is the inconsequential tune in the first movement:

Ex. 13

which not only recalls the falling shape of Ex. 12 but provides the thematic basis of an emotional outburst – also in E major – at the end of the *adagio*. This theme has elements of the subsequent melody of the concluding song. Close listening reveals many subtle and charming interconnections throughout the entire work, and it is easy to see that the mood and thematic motivation of the finale inspire the Symphony from its first cheerful sounds, a point first noted by Paul Bekker. The strophic song, 'Wir geniessen die himmlischen Freuden', offers a view of celestial life which cannot seem very convincing today. However, the music is delightful. Mahler approached the world of childhood's dreaming armed with sophisticated musical resources, and to a great extent the beauty of the music outstrips the *Wunderhorn* simplicity of the words so completely that an element of contradiction arises between the Symphony and the images which originally inspired it.

It is poetically appropriate that Mahler's last *Wunderhorn* symphony ends in E major – a key shared by such peaceful works as the Nocturne in Mendelssohn's *Midsummer Night's Dream* music, the two E major Preludes and Fugues in Bach's '48', and the slow movement of Beethoven's Op. 90 and Op. 109. The world of the *Wunderhorn,* richly idealised in Mahler's musical imagination, is left quietly behind. There are no more explicit references to or settings of the poems; but Mahler's musical mentality seems always to be motivated by a lyrical impulse which shaped itself again and again in melodic terms first consciously associated with the visionary world of Brentano and Arnim's collection. In the next three symphonies, Mahler entered upon a dialectical struggle, when he wrestled with musical conceptions which he tried to dissociate from non-musical conceptions. If the *Wunderhorn* phase reflects, on the whole, happiness, aspiration and Mahler's personal brand of humanised catholicism, the Fifth, Sixth and Seventh Symphonies project the pain and stress of a sensitive mind tried in the fire of mental suffering.

The Fifth, Sixth and Seventh Symphonies

Almost all Mahler's creative work was done during the late summer, when he enjoyed temporary freedom from the pressure of his professional duties as conductor. Considering the length and complexity of the symphonies, he must have worked at fever pitch merely to get the notes down on paper. However, having completed a score, he was unable to leave it alone. An inherently anxious, introverted temperament led him into endless revisions. There may have been an element of ruthless perfectionism in this; but it is equally likely that the composer's sensitivity to adverse criticism, his basic sense of insecurity exacerbated by unfavourable critical notices in Berlin, and difficulties with professional relationships all overflowed into anxieties about the quality of his work and made it impossible for him to leave a piece with a feeling of final satisfaction. The Fourth Symphony, for example, was published in 1901; but the composer was still revising it nine years later. The Fifth was revised again and again between 1907 and 1909. In the Sixth Mahler changed his mind about the relative positions of slow movement and scherzo. The Seventh was issued in a reasonably definitive form as late as 1962 in the Eulenburg edition.

The growth in maturity evident in the symphonies is tremendous, considering that they were all compressed into a relatively short period of time. The First was composed in 1894. Only ten years later Mahler was working on the Seventh, a composition of vastly different character in a much more advanced idiom. The Tenth was sketched in the summer of 1910, but left unfinished at his death. Between the years 1894 and 1910 Mahler therefore completed nine long symphonies and *Das Lied von der Erde*. During this period his musical style deepened in intensity, to mature into orchestral textures of wonderful colour, contrapuntal complexity characterised by strong, sinewy lines, astringent harmony frequently compounded of fourths and bare, pungent progressions, and unrivalled expressive power. His major works are largely free of obtrusive Wagnerian traits. Particularly striking are the clarity and strong colouring of his part-writing, and a kind of chromaticism which, although remarkably free in reaching out beyond implied basic harmonies, never loses itself in thick, wandering tonality. For Schoenberg and Alban Berg, Mahler was both an inspiration and a pointer to new developments, notwithstanding his wry self-criticism to the effect that he knew he was an old-fashioned composer. Mahlerian traits are obvious in the music of Shostakovich; and the influence upon Britten is well known, and openly acknowledged by him.

Despite Mahler's open disavowal of programmatic content there *are* associations. The first movement of the Sixth Symphony contains a theme (Ex. 16) which is supposed to be a portrait of Alma Mahler. The three hammer blows in the finale of the same work are said to 'lay the Titan to rest', although he had already had his funeral rites in the 'Resurrection' Symphony. The Fifth conforms suspiciously to the 'tragedy-despair-consolation-triumph' pattern, and the Seventh introduces thematic fragments from earlier *Wunderhorn* songs. The Fifth and Sixth Symphonies arouse strong reactions, either of admiration or dislike, as they did in Mahler's own day. The Seventh makes its way slowly and cannot be considered popular. Redlich remarked shrewdly that Mahler 'failed to convince even himself in this work'.

Symphonic wholeness, in Mahler's view, expressed in a conversation with Sibelius, who thought in terms of thematic integration and logical development, means the wholeness of a world. We have already noted thematic cross-references in the earlier symphonies; but Mahler's symphonic worlds are built up of tonal images which each reflect some aspect of experience. The primary unifying principle is psycho-spiritual, the subjective, suffering self, exploring heights and plunging into depths. It is precisely because the Seventh fails to achieve a unified world of tonal images that it remains relatively unconvincing as a whole. We might say that the Fifth and Sixth, for all their excursion into the realm of 'absolute music', with extended thematic development and transformation, succeed because they still conform to the 'world' conception. This is not to deny that the Seventh contains forward-looking music of great power and interest.

SYMPHONY NO. 5

The study of thematic structure in the Fifth Symphony (1902) immediately reveals familiar shapes related to Ex. 1, and these tend to recur increasingly in Mahler's later work. The first section is a funeral march, beginning with a 'fate' motive somewhat resembling the opening of Beethoven's Fifth. Its middle section (*Leidenschaftlich. Wild.*) is a tremendous outburst of desperation. The next movement, directed to be played with great vehemence, is really a fantasia upon the march – an elaboration recalling the long section linking 'Urlicht' with 'Auferstehen' in the Second Symphony. This is stormy music of disturbing force, exploiting and finally exhausting the mood of tragedy and desperation set in the opening movement, and ending in a chorale destined to find triumphant apotheosis in the finale. The scherzo is an intense though grotesque evocation of both *Ländler* and waltz. Viennese waltz melodies reveal great ingenuity in breaking up triple metre into standard rhythmical formations. In this movement Mahler explores all the standard patterns of triple dance-structure; but he concedes little to customary Viennese sweetness, infusing the rhythmic patterns with fiendish vitality and distorting the melodic line with awkward intervals, all the time drawing out thematic motives in a forced, asymmetrical extension. Until Mahler invented this kind of symphonic 'parody-*Ländler*', no Austrian could have heard his favourite rhythms treated so brutally. The frenzied, hectic effect arises from the fact that the associations of Viennese rhythm are thrown out of joint when traditional melodic and harmonic conventions are dislocated. In earlier Viennese dance music we find sequences of formally symmetrical tunes, frequently of great beauty and rhythmic subtlety; but the Strausses, and notably Josef, later developed the idiom by inventing asymmetrical melodies considerably extended by developmental and subsidiary figures and enhanced with adventurous modulation. Mahler was well aware of this, and had a deep, although concealed, admiration for Austrian waltzes and the world of operetta. However, he reinterpreted the idiom according to his own symphonic logic. The result, as Cardus picturesquely puts it, is that 'waltz rapes *Ländler*',* although it might be truer to say that Mahler raped both.

The celebrated *adagio* for harp and strings, sometimes taken out of context and played as a separate piece, is probably Mahler's best-known movement. It has frequently been used as incidental music for films and radio plays, and always at moments of romantic sorrow. The Rückert songs 'Ich bin der Welt abhanden gekommen' and 'Nun seh' ich wohl' contain melodic material found here. There is much dramatic inflection in the main theme which, however, repeatedly opens out in broad sweeps supported by solemn diatonic triads.

The popular rondo-finale begins with horn calls, answered by the bassoon which quotes a phrase from the *Wunderhorn* song 'Lob des hohen Verstandes':

Ex. 14

suggesting, incidentally, that although the *Wunderhorn* is supposedly out of the symphonic scheme, it can never be ignored. This points the irony of the movement. As the song is about a singing contest presided over by an ass, the polyphonic structure, which uses many contrapuntal devices, is placed by association in a strange context. Mahler here reveals his mastery in the world of pedants. Overall there is an abundance of thematic material, expounded in twenty

* Neville Cardus, *Gustav Mahler* (Gollancz, 1965).

preludial bars with much emphasis upon 'the ass's tail' – the falling figure at the end of Ex. 14. This appears in augmented form in many other thematic fragments, and is indeed a binding thread. It is used in retrograde formation and is virtually ubiquitous. Moreover it dovetails well into an important theme, alluding to the *adagio*, which follows preliminary contrapuntal exposition:

Ex. 15

The structure of the movement is extremely complex, and the combination of themes produces a busy texture. However, Mahler's muscular counterpoint generates considerable momentum and its powerful effect is supported by lucid orchestration highlighting different melodic strata. These strata are bound together in a fugal scheme and set in 'perpetual' motion by an irresistible march rhythm. Taken in isolation the separate themes may seem to lack distinction; but they embody just the kind of figuration which lends itself to contrapuntal development. The movement reaches an uplifting conclusion in a transformed version of the chorale theme first heard near the end of the second movement.

An overall feeling of tension in the Symphony arises from its progressive tonality. It begins in C sharp minor, and ends in D major; but it gets there via A minor (second movement) and F major (*adagio*), the scherzo being also in D. If these centres are synthesised in a chord, they produce a full major seventh with D as root. This is *not* to say that the Symphony grows out of this chord; but it is a striking symbol of the tension implicit in the whole scheme.

SYMPHONY NO. 6 IN A MINOR

The Sixth Symphony (1905), much revised since its performance at Essen in 1906, has not yet achieved the recognition it deserves. This may partly be because it stirs gloomy emotions without purging them. It worried even its composer, in whom it provoked deep agitation and melancholy introspection. It is in no sense an optimistic piece, and is perhaps all the greater as a work of art because it does not set out to propound facile solutions to the emotional stresses intensified in Mahler by the contemplation of life. Instead it works out these stresses in binding itself to logical symphonic procedures, and there is genius in the way these are developed to a conclusion.

The storm and stress of Mahler's Sixth Symphony arose from a deepening anxiety, an enduring spiritual concern which transmuted his intimate personal worries into sombre visions of the human condition. Such a transmutation explains the juxtaposition of anguished melody with detached interludes, emotional 'landscapes' where the panorama of feeling is temporarily held at arm's length and contemplated with an almost mystical detachment. It would be going much too far to suggest that Mahler ever really achieved Wordsworthian 'recollection of emotion in tranquillity' for more than short periods, if, indeed, at all; even his mystical detachment quickly flows into a bitter-sweet introspection. But in this Symphony he repeatedly withdraws from the more intense levels of subjective involvement. This withdrawal, which is certainly necessary in order to alleviate the more extreme rigours of emotional expression, is assisted by the use of cowbells, an imaginative colouristic device. All wanderers on the Alpine heights know this sound. The higher one ascends, the more remote the tintinnabulation, and the greater one's sense of detachment from the every-day world. According to temperament it can symbolise either a mystical freedom of the spirit, a closeness to God, or merely a feeling of loneliness and desolation. Throughout the work moods interpenetrate, conflict or combine, to be expressed in a vast structure of impressive proportions.

There are four movements, closely linked by common thematic elements and the major-minor chord relationship already invested with symbolic force in the Resurrection Symphony. The first movement begins with savage attack and presents material which assumes new importance in the scherzo. Here is the theme from the first movement which Alma claimed to be a musical portrait of herself:

Ex. 16

The *andante* is a lyrical interlude, a stream of dreaming melody recalling the familiar Mahler, the ecstatic song-writer who soon took up his romantic lyre again in the Eighth Symphony and *The Song of the Earth*. In the finale, thematic material is distorted by chromatic inflection and octave displacement:

Ex. 17

but most disturbing of all are the three hammer blows, each of which comes at the height of a developmental section.

This tragic work is perhaps Mahler's finest purely instrumental piece. Its central tonality, A minor, is clearly established and this, together with closely integrated thematic structure, reinforces its dynamic form. It is the most 'classical' of the composer's works. Both Schoenberg and Berg were deeply impressed by it, and Mahler's individual way of stretching out themes in asymmetrical lines and wide leaps anticipated later trends in expressionism.

It can be argued that classical tonality is a projection of the experiences of the self unconsciously identified with the tonic principle, and that in Mahler's music the 'hero', the suffering self of the emotional action, is identified also with certain harmonic and thematic nuclei. Hence the emotional vicissitudes of the 'hero' become one with recurring basic shapes, their distortions, transpositions, extensions and often tortuous contrapuntal developments, and with the ever-recurring major-minor antithesis which paradoxically offers a kind of harmonic indetermination as the ultimate centre of structural function and the correlative symbol of the divided consciousness so penetratingly described in Hegel's *Phenomenology*.* These musical sounds are indeed symbols, and the musical logic of the form is inseparable from the symbolic logic of the inward, psychological drama in which Mahler's own consciousness is always the central character, a soul divided between its own trials and purgations and its concern for the suffering human spirit. Sympathetic understanding of Mahler's deepening psycho-spiritual sensitivity is important in appraisal of his later work. Moreover, serious consideration of the idea just propounded can throw light upon the subsequent development of expressionism and Schoenberg's later twelve-note theory. In Schoenberg's development, the psycho-spiritual centre of the self – the 'suffering hero' of earlier romantic music – is progressively identified first with recurrent chromatic patterns, and finally with shapes originating in an archetypal series, the series being firstly their *unconscious* dynamic force and only secondly their conscious rationalisation. The force and persistence of shapes related to Ex. 1 in Mahler's music illustrates a primitive phase of this process. The basic shape as given is really a rationalisation of Mahler's dominant thematic drive. This must represent a correlative, subconscious urge with which his inner self was identified. Equally interesting, of course, is the fact that similar shapes appear elsewhere in romantic music, often with some common underlying association, and this suggests a significant preoccupation of late-romantic composers with a basic feeling archetypal in relation to the deepest levels of the romantic impulse itself.

SYMPHONY NO. 7

Concerning the Seventh Symphony (also completed in 1905),

* In *The Phenomenology of Spirit* Hegel wrote illuminatingly of *das unglückliche Bewusstsein* ('the unhappy consciousness') which is divided between self-knowledge of its own spiritual imperfections and an intuition of its divine destiny and selfhood.

Redlich notes that Mahler's tendency to self-repetition 'becomes apparent for the first time'. In fact, as we have seen, Mahler's reliance upon basic shapes used either more or less literally or incorporated as seed-elements in longer statements, or twisted and teased by chromatic extension into elaborate sentences anticipating the freer style of expressionism, suggests that Mahler had been quoting himself before this. If, in the Seventh Symphony, he was indeed reworking earlier inspirations, then there may well have been some psychological blockage, a weakening of inspiration evident to himself. In which case the deliberate invocation of inspiration in the Eighth Symphony is very significant.

Mahler himself had doubts about the Seventh. By the time it was ready for its first performance in Prague on 19 September 1908, the Eighth and *Das Lied von der Erde* were virtually complete, and the world of the Seventh had been left behind. Redlich points out in his introduction to the 1962 edition of the Eulenburg score that Mahler's doubts arose mainly from his own sense of stylistic syncretism. There is a tendency nowadays to extol the work for its forward-looking tendencies. Undoubtedly it contains splendid music; yet it does lack cohesion, because its three central movements do not agree stylistically with the first movement and finale. There is no real formal synthesis: the different movements do not, in sum, constitute a symphonic world according to the composer's own standards. The tonal scheme is unusual. The first movement begins *Langsam* (slowly) in B minor, to be followed by an *allegro con fuoco* beginning in E minor and ending in E major. The second movement – 'Night Music' (*allegro moderato*) – is pitched in C major and followed by a 'shadow-like' scherzo in D minor. The fourth movement, another *Nachtmusik* (*andante amoroso*), is in F major, and the rondo-finale, much resembling the rondo of the Fifth Symphony, is in C major.

The two outer movements of the Symphony clearly belong to the same world as the corresponding movements of the Fifth, and there is an analogous tonal relationship between them. The Fifth begins in C sharp minor, and the rondo in D major. In the Seventh, Mahler begins (at least) in B minor and ends in C major. Allowing that the tonal centre of the *allegro* is really E minor and major, then the second piece of *Nachtmusik*, in F major, has the same so-called 'Neapolitan' relation to it. The first *Nachtmusik* in C major is, like the concluding rondo, 'Neapolitan' to the B minor opening, and dominant to the second; while the scherzo in D minor is in the relative minor key of the second *Nachtmusik*. These semitonal relations loom strongly in the Fifth and Seventh Symphonies, and are also much exploited in the *andante* of the Sixth. When they occur between movements they create a sense of stress throughout an entire work. They are always haunting and dramatic.

Tonality apart, stylistic problems – arising from the fact that the three middle movements belong to a different world from that of the two outer ones – make the Seventh a somewhat bizarre experience. The affective tone of the *Nachtmusik* is that of the *Wunderborn*, although Mahler's retrospective glances have here a neurotic tinge, and there are no compelling links with the outer movements. Mahler described his difficulties to Alma in a letter dated June 1910. The *Nachtmusik* movements had already been written in the summer of 1904. A year later, after a summer void of inspiration, Mahler had an idea for the rhythm of the first movement, and soon had the first, third and fifth movements down on paper. The point here is that these sections are the result of a creative act quite separate from the inspiration of the Night Music.

Yet in the first movement, especially, there are visionary moments. The opening melody for tenor horn is one of the composer's most potent inspirations and it is magnificently worked up by other instruments into a prelude of symphonic grandeur. In the end, however, there is no escaping the sense of hiatus when the Night Music begins. Indeed, the second movement lasts too long for its slender, and indeed tedious, thematic material. Add to this the use of an important theme in the first movement which closely resembles the main theme of the first movement of the Sixth Symphony, reliance upon the overworked device of major-minor transformations, and protracted developmental procedures in the finale, and the conviction grows that this work fails to sustain a consistent level of interest.

Symphony No. 8

The Eighth Symphony, sometimes also called 'The Symphony of a Thousand' because of the huge resources it requires, is the last work Mahler ever conducted. It was composed in the summer of 1906, a year before he knew about the heart disease which eventually killed him. The task of composition took eight weeks precisely. The full significance of the work has still to be appreciated, even though the musical idiom presents no difficulties and in many places makes use of somewhat conventional, and even deliberately archaic, material, and it is very possible that Mahler's visions and aspirations anticipate a spiritual reawakening which still lies in the future of mankind. For in this tremendous choral symphony Mahler affirmed and deepened the Christian experience of faith and the Goethean image of the Feminine as a redemptive aspect of God. In doing this he abandoned the ideal of 'absolute music' and returned to the concept of sound as bearer of the *idea*. This means that performance of the Symphony is a ritual act, confronting the listener's mind with mystical images and concepts relating to the inner life of the soul.

Before the composition of the Eighth, Mahler had undoubtedly felt some diminution of inspiration. He hit upon the idea of symbolically invoking it by setting the medieval hymn of Hrabanus Maurus, 'Veni Creator Spiritus', which is not only beautiful in its Latin but heart-stirring in its direct and impassioned address to the Creator. In this famous prayer, more than a thousand years old, inspiration is invoked in the mind and heart, the two centres of our being associated with intellect and emotion through which Christians have sought illumination and mediated love. Mahler's musical utterance is here no merely passive contemplation of an idea: it is a strongly willed plea for a renewal of the inward fire from the source of all life and light. Moreover, and significantly, it is made against negative forces at work in himself. There are passages in the first movement which clearly indicate the collapse of faith, the bitterness of spiritual failure. It often seems that the closer Mahler came to doubt, and the more he suffered a generalised feeling of insecurity and anxiety, the more he exalted the notion of salvation for himself and mankind in transcendental visions.

The second movement, of enormous length, sets the last scene of the Second Part of Goethe's *Faust*. This famous scene is wholly symbolic, and it culminates in a vision of the Mater Gloriosa, Margaret's pardon and her insight into the true nature of the redeemed and regenerated Faust, and the culmination of their relationship when she is enjoined to lead Faust on to the higher spheres of being. The Symphony ends with Mahler's superb setting of the Chorus Mysticus, in which the symbolic nature of earthly life and the true significance for mankind of the feminine image are revealed. As Bayard Taylor, an early translator of *Faust,* commented:

Love is the all-uplifting and all-redeeming power on Earth and in Heaven; and to Man it is revealed in its most pure and perfect form through Woman. Thus, in the transitory life of Earth, it is only a symbol of its diviner being; the possibilities of Love, which Earth can never fulfil, become realities in the higher life which follows; the Spirit, which Woman interprets to us here, still draws us upward as Margaret draws the soul of Faust). . . .*

In a letter to Alma, written in June 1910, Mahler discusses Platonic love:

The essence of it is really Goethe's idea that all love is generative, creative, and that there is a physical and spiritual generation which is the emanation of this 'Eros'. You have it in the last scene of *Faust,* presented symbolically . . .

In the same letter he reveals his earlier interest in Plato's *Symposium.* Throughout his creative life he had been aware of the central doctrine of that work, which is crowned with the wonderful words of Diotima reported by Socrates, to the effect that love may be progressively sublimated until it manifests in the highest consciousness of the philosopher's contemplation of beauty. Mahler's letter is profoundly interesting in the context of his life at that time, for in the summer of 1910, after returning from America, he had visited Freud. He had also become tragically aware of the young Walter Gropius's interest in his wife, after reading a letter from him addressed in error. Freud accused Mahler of projecting love for his mother upon Alma, and pointed out that Alma, who had been devoted to her father, was attracted to Mahler precisely on account of something Mahler most feared – his age. Alma claimed that Freud was right in both cases. However, although on the surface there appears to be substance in Freud's diagnosis, Mahler, according to Alma, 'refused to acknowledge his fixation

* See Goethe's *Faust I* & *II* (Oxford, World's Classics).

upon his mother. He turned away from notions of that kind.' It may well be that Mahler could not look truth in the face. On the other hand, it is possible that the Freudian explanation was ultimately no explanation in the light of what he already knew about himself. Relevant to this subject, the jargon of which has passed into facile usage in our own time, is Jung's theory of the archetypal feminine, taken up again by Owen Barfield in a discussion of 'the intellectual soul':

One might almost say that the Ego in Central Europe lives always at the point of incarnation, and the Intellectual Soul is that point. . . . And it is to the culture of Central Europe that we in the West must look if we would find the actual concrete *meaning* of life – the living heart of nature – the Eternal Feminine.*

In the Eighth Symphony Mahler perfectly manifests this consciousness of 'the intellectual soul'. Yet, through the very force of emotional attraction on the one hand, and spiritual insecurity on the other, he seemed to fall back from the innermost meaning of that which both his musical imagination and philosophical intuition had grasped. After the vision of the Mater Gloriosa, which he ecstatically enshrined in ravishing music, he reverted to the passionate idealisation of his own wife, often in the most touching letters and poems:

Freud is quite right – you were always for me the light and the central point! The inner light, I mean, which rose over all; and the blissful consciousness of this – now unshadowed and unconfined – raises my feelings to the infinite.†

But Christian mysticism and Jungian psychology are at one in recognising the deviation from psychological stability inherent in such projections upon others. Eros itself has to be transcended. Even the image of the Mater Gloriosa is but a symbol, a gateway – the 'Eastern Gate' as Roman Catholic mysticism has called Her – through which consciousness passes to an ineffable mystery.‡ For Mahler the final confrontation with reality came through sorrow and loss, superbly expressed in the Ninth and Tenth Symphonies and in *Das Lied von der Erde*.

* *Romanticism Comes of Age* (Rudolf Steiner Press, 1944).
† Letter dated 4 September 1910.
‡ The Book of Ezekiel, Ch. 44, v. 2.

It is essential to listen to Mahler's music in the context of the basic *idea* which underlies the inspiration of the Eighth Symphony. This is conveyed in the remarkable juxtaposition of the 'Veni Creator Spiritus' with the *Faust* scene. The old prayer *invokes* inspiration, brings it *down,* so to speak, into mind and heart, and even literally into the physical body as a generative agent, which Mahler clearly understood. Yet spiritual psychology recognises that the force which has descended must reascend. What has come down to earth as grace has to be raised up to heaven through a progressive sublimation of energies. The physical life is transmuted through the heart's aspiration and a spiritual rebirth follows the transmutation of Eros. The sign of this rebirth is a vision of the Mater Gloriosa, Goethe's composite image of Isis and the Virgin Mary. Mahler's Symphony is a proclamation of faith in the transmutation of Eros into its highest spiritual expression, and the music unfolds as a procession of symbols pointing the way to an ideal concept of love. The culmination of its vision, the appearance of the Mater Gloriosa, and the choral setting of Goethe's final statement that all our experience here on earth is symbolic, both point unmistakably to a redemption of human sexuality and a regeneration of human life. In the Eighth Symphony, Mahler rejects that interpretation of Freudian psychology which denigrates the highest religious and poetic insights achieved in western civilisation. The Symphony tacitly proclaims and expresses the composer's life long ideal, the unity of art and revelation. When he joined the two texts in a single musical conception, Mahler added the force of artistic genius to a prophetic rejection of what passes for the sexual 'enlightenment' of our own era.

The Symphony is scored for a vast collection of instruments, including harmonium and mandolin, and for double choir, boys' choir and eight soloists. It is bound together by thematic cross-references and figures often showing family resemblance to Ex.1. There are pages, especially towards the end, where such figures seem to permeate every bar, and the music of the Mater Gloriosa gives them ecstatic expression. We may feel that they constitute sound-symbols ever associated in Mahler's subconscious mind with emotional aspiration and spiritual yearning.

Part I is approximately in sonata-form, with a condensed recapitulation. The development section eventually builds up into a massive double-fugue. The polyphonic structure is conceived along archaic lines matching the Latin text, and its overall effect is austere, with the exception of a passage in D minor, at the end of the exposition and continued into the development, which returns to Mahler's familiar vein of tortured introspection.

The work opens, *allegro impetuoso*, with tremendous force, fortissimo, on the following statement:

Ex. 18

Ve - ni, Ve - ni, Cre - a - tor Spi - ri - tus!

and this is followed immediately by trombones playing a variant:

Ex. 19

and violins with a figure inverting the important opening intervals, although with some freedom:

Ex. 20

Special notice should be taken of the dotted figure setting the word 'Spiritus', for it is a rhythmic element reappearing in other important themes. Further figures are contributed by tenor and soprano in a confident lyrical flow; but it is at the words 'Infirma nostri corporis' that this confident mood collapses into Mahlerian depression, as the composer contemplates human frailty. The passage turns to bitterness and despair; but a dramatic change occurs with modulation to E major (associated in the Second Symphony, it will be remembered, with an emotional clearing of the air) and

D

the whole orchestra and all the singers then give out the following ecstatic theme in the plea for light and love:

Ex. 21

Ac - cen - de, ac - cen-de lu – men sen-si – bus lu –

– men sen - si - bus, sen ʒ si – bus, ac - cen - de sen - si - bus.

After this the boys' choir sings 'Infunde amorem cordibus' to yet another theme revealing familiar elements – 'a carol-like song of joy', as Deryck Cooke has called it. As the texture evolves, earlier material derived from Ex. 19 acts like a binding thread. This evolution takes in vigorous march rhythms ('Hostem repellas longius') and the powerful double fugue, also in march tempo. In the condensed recapitulation the mood of spiritual optimism is preserved and the movement reaches a triumphant and breathtaking conclusion.

Part II makes a tremendous attempt to encompass in musical terms the ascent of consciousness through terraces of mystical apprehension. Goethe indicates a scene somewhat resembling the Dantean Mount of Paradise, with its heights reaching into the empyrean. All the singers are symbolical characters, 'singing ideas', and they correlate in the main with the progressive unfolding of spiritual awareness through penitence (Margaret), forgiveness and redemption (the three Marys), ecstasy (Pater Ecstaticus), intellectual insight (Pater Profundus), and that special vein of spiritual idealisation finding expression in the song of Dr Marianus, who, as his name implies, is dedicated to the Mater Gloriosa.

The music in which the unfolding grades of awareness are expressed falls into three substantial sections: *adagio, allegro* (with frequent variations of tempo) and finale. If the *allegro* is regarded as a scherzo, the Symphony approximates to the conventional four-movement outline. There is, however, a noticeable difference of style between Part I and the three-section Part II which, considered overall, is composed in a loose rhapsodic manner. The formal structure of the *allegro* is extremely free, and not entirely satisfactory in effect. Mahler had the problem of integrating choruses of boys together with solo music for Dr Marianus into a purposive, forward-moving texture. The problem recurs with the music for the three Marys in the final part. But the beautiful theme associated with the Mater Gloriosa (Ex. 22 below) gives the unifying inspiration which enables Mahler to knit everything together. The chorus swells wave upon wave in slow, measured rhythm to unfold some of the loveliest music he ever wrote.

Part II opens with sounds related to the 'Accende' theme depicting the symbolic mountain of anchorites. Its melodic extension is a prominent feature throughout. Related to it is an anticipation of the music of Pater Ecstaticus; and there are new figures later to be associated with Pater Profundus. The movement unfolds with a chorus of anchorites and solos for the two Fathers. Pater Profundus brings his song to a climax of expressive declamation with material derived from the 'Accende' theme which, with subtle transformations, subsequently forms the basis of the finale. The symbolic cross-referencing is clear. The original 'Accende' theme is a plea for love and illumination. With much the same figure, Pater Profundus prays in the depths of an encompassing darkness for light and love. Finally, refined still further into a melody of ethereal beauty, this root figure is linked with a vision of the Mater Gloriosa.

The middle section brings angels into view carrying the immortal part of Faust. 'Blessed boys', who appear to symbolise innocent, because unincarnated, consciousness, add their chorus of praise, and 'younger angels' introduce a new theme and symbolic references to 'roses' which have the power to repel evil. This, and a cryptic reference to 'Asbestos' in the song of 'the more perfect angels', reveals, like many other mysterious allusions in *Faust,* a depth of symbolism in Goethe's work which it is possible that Mahler himself did not understand. The likelihood is that he did not; and it is certain that these strange lines did not call forth his most convincing music.

The climax of the Symphony is initiated by a beautiful violin theme heard above an E major chord on harp and harmonium after the enraptured song of Dr Marianus:

Ex. 22

This marks the beginning of the final section, which now introduces the chorus, the three penitents, Margaret's address to the Mater Gloriosa, the chorus of the 'blessed boys' and the Mater Gloriosa herself. Perhaps the most beautiful moments in the entire work are when Dr Marianus greets the Queen of Heaven, urging the penitents to gaze aloft as the chorus beckons them – and, by implication, the whole of mankind – onwards and upwards to the highest spheres of being. It is an injunction of inexhaustible significance, and Mahler responds to it with soaring melody which touches the highest peaks of romantic art.

The famous Chorus Mysticus, affirming the mystical transcendence of the Feminine – which is, after all, God apprehended through the grace of the feminine image instead of that of the wrathful Jehovah – begins with a whisper and ends in a blaze of glory.

Mahler's masterstroke is to bring back the 'Veni Creator Spiritus' theme at the end of the instrumental coda; but its initial interval of the seventh is now transformed into a major ninth by trumpets and trombones blazing through E flat harmony like a triumphant flame. Thus, they seem to say, that which descends into the substance of man must reascend through man to complete the work of the manifesting spirit.

The Last Phase

The year 1907 was a major turning-point. In July of that year, after the death of his elder daughter, a visiting doctor revealed to Mahler that he had contracted a fatal heart disease. The inevitable effect was a plunge into despair; yet it was from the very substance of bitter and tragic premonitions that Mahler conceived his greatest work, *Das Lied von der Erde,* and the Ninth Symphony which, in part at least, is music of sombre power and grandeur. *Das Lied* was finished in October 1909, and the Ninth Symphony in March 1910, when Mahler was in New York. Another symphony, the Tenth, was begun in 1910 but left unfinished.

These last works were composed against a background of travel and emotional disturbance. Following intrigue at the Vienna Opera, Mahler relinquished his post there and accepted a conductorship at the Metropolitan Opera in New York. During the last four years of his life he made four visits to America, on the second of which (1908–9) he was appointed conductor of the new Philharmonic Society of New York. After his third trip he visited Freud at Leyden; and it is entirely due to the researches of Donald Mitchell that some of the facts of that interview have come to light. It must have been one of the most interesting conversations in the history of psychiatry. But the developing illness – and it was now a question of both physical and emotional imbalance, combined with deteriorating relations with his American orchestra – brought about a fatal collapse. Mahler was brought back to Europe in April 1911. He died in Vienna on 18 May during a a thunderstorm. Alma records that he read philosophical works to the end, the last being E. von Hartmann's *The Problem of Life*.

Mahler scaled tremendous heights in the Eighth Symphony. Yet shortly afterwards the pendulum swung to the other extreme. Earlier he had mysteriously, if superstitiously, suspected a connection between the subjective energies of musical composition and events in the outer world. The *Kindertotenlieder* had been composed at a time when he had nothing to fear but fear itself. Then his elder daughter had died, choked with diphtheria. In a similar spirit, and with more reason, Mahler felt himself doomed, and shied away from performance of *Das Lied* and the funereal Ninth Symphony. He considered *Das Lied,* which is really an orchestral song-cycle, a symphony, to persuade himself that the true Ninth was really his Tenth. Schubert, Beethoven, Bruckner and Dvořák all died after composing nine symphonies. So, tragically, did Mahler. The Tenth remains an inspired fragment, although Deryck Cooke has made a complete version which brilliantly develops the implications of the sketches with a deep insight into Mahler's style and methods.

DAS LIED VON DER ERDE

The literary inspiration for *The Song of the Earth* derives from Hans Bethge's German translations of old Chinese poetry. Bethge's anthology appeared in 1908, and from it Mahler selected seven poems, two of which were fused in the last movement of the cycle, 'Der Abschied' (Farewell). Their overall theme is familiar enough: the transitoriness of all things, the passing joys of youth and beauty, the loneliness of the soul confronting life in all its mystery, consolation in nature and wine, the wraith-like, fading moods of the soul, and a general feeling for quiet lakes, mists and distant hills. The far horizons of the beautiful Earth are intimations of a vision ever unfulfilled in the sad enigma of human experience. The happiness of earlier days becomes a memory, a pain, a wound in the heart, a receding horizon promising nothing. For most listeners, the music is most eloquent in the heart-breaking 'Abschied'. Here consciousness itself dissolves in a blue remoteness. The wanderer leaves Earth and life for ever, and the joy of the seasons is no more.

Analysis of the thematic material reveals significant echoes of the Eighth Symphony, the spiritual optimism of which has now been darkened by the confrontation with death. Here the recent exaltation of 'Accende lumen sensibus' falters in the dreaming sadness of the last farewell:

Ex. 23

Ecstatic visions of the Eternal Feminine have not found earthly expressions in the composer's life. The ideal beckoned, the 'intellectual soul' glimpsed heights of spiritual grandeur; but for many listeners it must seem that despair and hopeless nostalgia made worse by an increasing anxiety state and excessive introspection are the predominant characteristics of the last works, and especially the Tenth Symphony, the score of which is marked by hysterical scribblings.

Das Lied expresses resignation to loss. Does Mahler, perhaps, achieve maturity as a composer in precisely this? The final mood of resignation calls forth his finest and most enduring music. And as a man, whose creative energies had previously been expended to a great extent in the expression of ideals and aspirations, he now seemed to find some peace in relinquishing them. Behind the melancholy of *The Song* lurks a new consciousness, a psychological perception which had hitherto found no musical expression. Inspired by Bethge's translations, Mahler, like Bethge himself, brings through a quality of awareness truly reflecting a significant aspect of the Oriental mind. It has been said that whereas the Western mind is orientated towards consciousness, the Eastern is centred in the unconscious. The unconscious everywhere pervades *Das Lied von der Erde*. The very state of conscious attention engendered by the music paradoxically reflects the ocean of unconsciousness. Everything is heard and experienced as if it is being remembered. The sounds themselves, especially the seemingly disembodied contralto voice at the end, all polarise the mind in a world of stillness, shadowy images, a mirror emptying itself of all forms. The very sound of Mahler's orchestra dissolves the flow of images.

All this finally condenses into the pathos of the word 'ewig' which Mahler sets to the falling step E–D in the closing bars. We have already noticed his significant use of the falling step in connection with the Nietzsche setting in the Third Symphony, and in the first movement of the Ninth. Hans Redlich has also drawn attention to symbolic use of the same device in the Ninth, and likened it to Beethoven's 'Lebewohl' in the piano sonata, Op. 81a. Mahler's quotation, if such it is, seems to be explicit at the end of the first movement in the Ninth Symphony; but his pathos is immeasurably deeper. In his case there was to be no return. The falling tone also recurs in a heartfelt passage of bitter irony about a third of the way through the same movement, where Mahler refers to a waltz by Johann Strauss the younger, called *Freut euch des Lebens* ('Enjoy life'), Op. 340:

Ex. 24

Indeed, the falling step, whether expressed as a whole tone or bridged by a chromatic note, is a hallmark of Mahler's musical style. It is often associated with an incomplete, unfulfilled feeling, most clearly conveyed in the final 'ewig' of 'Der Abschied', and it aptly reverses the characteristic upward curve of melodies in other works associated with aspiration and optimism.

'Das Trinklied vom Jammer der Erde' ('Drinking song of the sorrow of the earth') is one of Mahler's finest musical structures. It is set for tenor, and the orchestra is large, though frequently broken down into small, colourful groupings. The opening horn call has a note of urgency and desperation, soon developed by the singer. The most impressive stroke is Mahler's setting of the phrase: 'Dunkel ist das Leben, ist der Tod' ('Dark is life, dark is death'). It appears three times, raised a semitone in its second and third utterances. The last statement restores the tonic A minor. 'Der Einsame im Herbst' ('The lonely one in autumn'), played 'somewhat dragging, wearily', and sung by contralto, is based upon figures drawn from a simple pentatonic shape and a drifting quaver accompaniment. Its apparent shapelessness, although both the melodic and harmonic movement are worked out with sure insight, magically evokes the spirit of loneliness, desolation and finality. Loveliest of all is the episode in D major 'Ich komm' zu dir, traute Ruhestätte!', which is an inverse form of the basic shape quoted in Ex. 1.

In the three middle movements, 'Von der Jugend' (Of Youth),

sung by tenor, 'Von der Schönheit' (Of Beauty), sung by contralto, and 'Der Trunkene im Frühling' (The drunkard in spring), tenor, the mood is livelier but certainly not happy. The images evoked are images of states past so far as Mahler is concerned, mere shadows in the unconscious which holds them motionless in contemplation. And the miracle of the music is that throughout the interplay of rich colours and subtle rhythms, sound merely deepens the sense of contemplative stillness in the mind's ear. Nothing really moves. All is retrospective.

The true spiritual centre of the work, the unconscious abyss of the soul which contemplates its inevitable withdrawal from the world, is deeply and finally affirmed in 'Der Abschied'. From A major, the key of the previous song, the harmony shifts to C minor. Deep, solemn tones reverberate in the void, and a plangent oboe plays a turn, a simple but telling device with an affective tone binding the whole movement together. The harmony is stark, and the scoring merely opens up hollow vastnesses, creating a sense of spiritual emptiness distantly recalling the effect of the shepherd's tune at the opening of the Third Act of *Tristan*. Repeated thirds have a remorseless, measured tread. The voice enters like a stranger adrift in infinite space, after a solitary low C has sounded its message of dissolution. As previously mentioned, there is thematic connection with the song 'Ich bin der Welt abhanden gekommen'.

A new section begins with a shift to F major, when the oboe sings a sad melody above an expressive harp and clarinet accompaniment characterised by a subtle rhythmic counterpoint:

Ex. 25

There is a very similar passage in the slow finale of the Ninth Symphony which, although purely orchestral, echoes the overall feeling of 'Der Abschied'. Here again harp and clarinet are used in much the same accompanimental figure, resounding through a passage of heart-stirring sadness and beauty:

Ex. 26

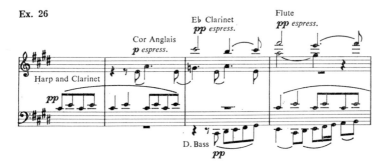

It is worth remembering that the same musico-poetic idea was embodied in the fourth *Wayfarer* song and in the slow movement of the First Symphony. In the last pages of 'The Farewell', the final sounds of what is Mahler's most perfect work, the contralto voice floats in an ethereal space, poised like the moon above silent seas. Its long-drawn melody proclaims that Mahler has found a definitive mode of lyrical expression.

SYMPHONY NO. 9

Alban Berg wrote enthusiastically to his fiancée of the death-conscious music of the Ninth Symphony, and revealed much insight into it. The fine first movement is sombre and terrifying. Redlich has pointed out that it mirrors a psychological struggle with death, depicted in the alternation of slow, plangent textures with passages of feverish tension. Mahler's life-long ambivalent relationship with Richard Strauss is illuminated by a comparison between this movement and the first part of Strauss's *Death and Transfiguration*. Strauss's imagination plays on the physical factors, and the outcome of the death-struggle seems naive; Mahler's music is infinitely more profound, for the struggle, after all, is an experienced one taking place in the substance of his own spirit.

The next movement, a tedious and far too expansive *Ländler*, does not rivet the listener's attention like the first. Its main thematic substance is a trivial commonplace of the Viennese idiom, and it is not redeemed by the burden of development it has to bear. The massive extension of the movement, through derivative and subsidiary material, seems an artistic miscalculation.

The *Rondo-Burleske* is savage and uncompromising, even vicious in its contrapuntal acerbity. The pace is remorseless and it reveals the burning creative energy locked up in Mahler's symphonic conception. Some of the material on which the lovely concluding *adagio* is based already occurs here. The *adagio* itself is a hymn-like soliloquy ending in a mood of sadness and remoteness.

In mood and structure the two outer movements echo *Das Lied,* and the slow movement particularly has close affinities with 'The Farewell' (Ex. 26). The Symphony deepens introspective meditation to an overwhelming pitch, and the almost claustrophobic melancholy of the first movement, unlike *Das Lied,* offers no panoramic images, no text to broaden the horizon of contemplation beyond the narrowing perspective of an acutely suffering soul. There is even an inverse mysticism here, an ecstasy of despair, a unity not with the creative fullness and richness of life – as in the Third Symphony – but with the abyss in which all forms dissolve. The disintegrative process contemplated by the composer within his own being is mirrored in the structure of the first movement, which introduces halting, broken phrases, fragmented figures, hesitant rhythms.

Quotations from the first movement and finale have already been given (Ex. 11 (ii), 24 and 26). The texture is complex. A great deal is going on, and only careful listening and repeated hearings will reveal its subtleties. Particularly noteworthy are the plangent sounds of the harp in the opening bars, which show an unconventional but wonderfully effective use of that instrument; whereas the menacing drum rolls constantly darken and rumble through the orchestral tapestry. The ironic quotation from Johann Strauss (Ex. 24) exhibits a familiar shape – rising sixth from dominant to mediant followed by gradual descent to the tonic. The dying fall mediant – supertonic – tonic is a common element in German romantic melody frequently exploited for nostalgic and melancholy effects. Compare, for example, the *Lebewohl* ('Farewell') theme from Beethoven's Piano Sonata, Op. 81a, and, in this symphony, the final *adagio,* where the opening melody introduces it twice in two profoundly expressive bars. The diatonic steps of the hymn-like first theme, introduced by a curving preludial phrase on unison violins, are quickly subjected to chromatic intensification, as if to prepare for a second, heavily inflected theme, which heightens the mood of desperate sadness. As the movement unfolds, the preludial turn becomes more important, and is used as a key figure binding the texture together. It is given to the viola in the last whispered bars. Subjective reactions to this haunting music must inevitably differ; but the passage in the middle of the movement beginning with Ex. 26 is surely one of Mahler's loveliest, if saddest, inspirations.

SYMPHONY NO. 10 (UNFINISHED)

The *andante-adagio* of the Tenth Symphony is often played as a separate piece. It is the first of the planned five-movement work. Also, it is the only movement completed by Mahler in full score. There were to have been at least three scherzo-like movements developing the savage, Mephistophelian style of the scherzo of the Fifth and the *Rondo-Burleske* of the Ninth Symphonies. None of these movements reached a musical conception beyond the sketch stage, and even the famous slow movement would certainly have been thoroughly revised by the composer, who always continued revising his work long after the first publication. As Erwin Ratz points out, in his introduction to the 1964 edition, Schoenberg, Berg, Webern and Křenek, all of whom knew Mahler's sketches well, declined to touch them. In their view, the work had not reached a stage in Mahler's conception when others could confidently predict his intentions. However, Deryck Cooke has attempted to do so. And it may well be that when one tries to penetrate the mind of a dead composer, subconscious energies and insights can guide one's pen.

The deep anguish in which Mahler began work on the Symphony is clearly apparent in the allusions scrawled on the score, and of course in the *adagio*, which is music of strange and terrifying intensity. The title of the sketched third movement was to have been 'Purgatorio', which gives a literary clue to the Dantean visions and apprehensions which overwhelmed Mahler's imagination during his last hours of creative work. It could be argued that despite evocative movements in earlier music which convey impressions of blue skies and green fields (though seldom without a touch of nostalgia) Mahler had all his life sought to use the world of sound to penetrate beyond the veil of earthly life. Again and again, in many a nostalgic song, in religious aspiration to resurrection and redemption, in heavenly visions, in dark-toned funeral marches, or in premonitory lamentations and shattering symphonic assaults, Mahler had tonally envisaged death. In Lawrence Gilman's telling phrase, Mahler had literally 'feasted and banqueted on death'. Now death stood before him; and there are moments in the *adagio* when he achieves an expressionistic breakthrough, when the 'tonal psychism' reaches such a pitch of appalling intensity that the power of sound alone seems to shatter the veil between life and death. No form of words can convey anything of the experience locked up in the terrifying shrieks which erupt *fff* from a *ppp* background at the climax of this movement. In this music emotional crisis proves its power to awaken psychic apprehensions, even if these are tonally and not visually experienced. Scribbled on the original sketches pathetic exclamations ('Mercy! O Lord! Why hast Thou forsaken me?') and despairing references to his wife ('Farewell, my lyre') reveal a mind already separated from the living, in which spiritual consolation has been occluded by terror and agonising emotions arising from a hopeless sense of loss.

Mahler's mind, *in extremis,* is a microcosm of the romantic-expressionistic crisis in the early years of the twentieth century, a crisis suffered also by Schoenberg, and to some extent by Berg and Webern. From it emerged the aesthetic of twelve-note music which reimposed order upon the chaotic flux of raging emotions expressed in a disembodied chromaticism – disembodied because the positive force of the old tonal centre, the classical centre of gravity in which the musical consciousness had hitherto found its creative identity, had dissolved in free harmonic clusters and wandering chromatic inflections.

The first sounds of the Symphony, fifteen *andante* bars for violas unaccompanied, are prophetic:

Ex. 27

The melody is drawn out in virtually free chromatic rhapsody, whereas the main theme of the *adagio*:

Ex. 28

is subsequently inverted and played in counterpoint against itself. This inspired and forward-looking movement inevitably provokes speculation. What would the finished work have been like? The fact remains that its remarkable musical idiom was born of the immediacy of confrontation with death. Had this sense of immediacy not been the keynote of Mahler's consciousness at this time, the raw nerves of his last music could not have been so painfully exposed.

To savour fully the substance of the Tenth Symphony, and the amazing musical development it represents, the listener should look back to the *Wunderhorn* symphonies, comparing their diatonic melodies with the chromatic expressionism of Mahler's unfinished score. Musical and psychological development should be considered together.

The *adagio* is music of astounding intensity, expanding awareness to the abyss in which all our thoughts, actions, hopes and aspirations seem diminished to the status of idle fantasy. For anyone who loves the Mahler of the *Wunderhorn* music, it is a profoundly uncomfortable experience, almost a study in the disintegration of consciousness expressed in the disruption of tonicity, groping chromaticism and spine-chilling sound-colours which awaken turbulent apprehension. There is nothing remotely consoling about this music, despite passages of concentrated sweetness which seem to parody the composer's earlier lyrical manner. It may be doubted whether even the later expressionists made instrumental sounds carry such a powerful burden. The essence of the texture is a long-drawn-out thread of melody characterised by the intuitive association of chromatic intervals. Points of sound are tenuously linked by chromatic relations dictated by intense feeling, and they do not require justification as 'enhancements' of conventional progressions. Linear construction, motivated by an intense emotional drive, and not at all by purely abstract or 'mathematical' calculation in the manner of more recent experiments, is here freeing itself from the familiar steps of the seven-point scale and the more familiar modulatory and chromatic elaboration of that scale characteristic of romantic harmony generally. Hence arise patterns and shapes characterised by angular 'corners', unexpected twists and octave displacement giving rise to wide leaps. The effect of octave displacement in particular is to isolate melodic notes within their linear context, and to emphasise their intrinsic value as intense stabs of feeling. Through such highly imaginative developments Mahler, in the context of his own time, seems no longer 'an old-fashioned composer', but one who takes his place in the history of twentieth-century music. He opened up new and significant worlds of musical experience, bringing the listener into a confrontation with musical vistas arising from contact with inner levels of thought and feeling which earlier phases of romanticism had scarcely touched. Today his music is more than ever relevant, because it achieves a powerful synthesis of tonal movement with the life of the mind and emotions. It belongs to a mental world which modern man knows now only too well.

There is plenty of internal evidence in the earlier works that Mahler was acutely sensitive to the human condition in a way characteristic of an intensely religious mind which found difficulty in accepting conventional frameworks of belief. He seemed deeply aware of the need for a new dispensation, a new consciousness, a newer insight into the mystery of the universe than that offered by traditional Christianity as he knew it, or the romantic-religious mysticism diffused through German philosophy after Hegel. Above all, his mind had seized upon the terrifying fact that the context of human experience is really limitless – that is, it is not bounded by the immediately visible world of everyday things. Our 'here' is, in truth, the everywhere of space; our situation, the real context of our life and action, is a moment in what Hegel, deeply moved by the panorama of human suffering, had called 'the slaughter-bench of human history'. Hence the 'nocturnal element' in Mahler's music. When the sun sets, the abyss is revealed by millions of remote stars. When the mind, seeking the meaning of life, turns inwards, what does it find? A subjective abyss full of uncertainties and unknowables! 'The night is deep, and deeper than the day thinks,' warns Zarathustra, an observation Mahler had certainly taken to heart.

It was in the context of spiritual anxiety arising from such realisations that Mahler passionately sought confirmation of his belief in God. A man can believe, and act upon that belief; but he may be challenged to maintain belief in the persistent absence of subjective illumination, and even in the face of apparent rejection, despair and death. The struggle of the composer's highly emotional temperament with the problem of belief is revealed in the urgent way he addresses his own soul in the last movement of the Second Symphony: 'O glaube, mein Herz, O glaube!' In Mahler's last music, the problem is not resolved. Taken as a whole, his symphonies mark stages on an incomplete spiritual journey, the end of which cannot be grasped in this life. They reach out musically, emotionally, philosophically, towards a spiritual order believed in and richly imagined. But there are movements which reflect a wavering, a falling back, irony and mistrust. Almost the whole of the Sixth Symphony is one sombre and bitter struggle – and all the more significant because there are no texts to underline any specific idea. In the unfinished Tenth Symphony, we hear the music of a man whose belief in spiritual reality is being tested to destruction.